1791

THE OBSERVER

Sayings of the Week

Selected and compiled by
Valerie Ferguson

David & Charles Newton Abbot London
North Pomfret (Vt)

British Library Cataloguing in Publication Data

Sayings of the week.
1. Quotations, English
I. Ferguson, Valerie   II. 'Observer, The'
828'.9'140208   PN6081

ISBN 0 7153 7600 4

Library of Congress Catalog Card Number 78-62483

First published 1978
Second impression November 1978

Set in Monotype Ehrhardt
and printed in Great Britain
by Western Printing Services, Bristol
for David & Charles (Publishers) Limited
Brunel House Newton Abbot Devon

Published in the United States of America
by David & Charles Inc
North Pomfret Vermont 05053 USA

Introduction

The day of the jewelled epigram is past and, whether one likes it
or not, one is moving into the stern puritanical era of the four-
letter word.

Lord Annan 20.2.1966

If you read an article you agree with, you think 'Aha!' You
don't think 'I agree with the writer' but 'the writer agrees with
me.' The key to success is the Aha Syndrome.

Stanhope Shelton 5.10.1969

'You should say what you mean,' the March Hare went on.
'I do,' Alice hastily replied; 'at least I mean what I say—that's
the same thing you know.'

Lewis Carroll, Alice in Wonderland

The Observer has published Sayings of the Week since
January 1917—a total of 21,179 to the end of December 1977.
They may be wise or witty, pompous, portentous or just
plain dotty, but each one should have a distinct flavour of the
time. In their entirety they show a panorama of the last
sixty-one years that is as intriguing as a view through a
camera obscura, as astonishing and nostalgic as an old photo-
graph album.

I have aimed at a small selection that is both representative
and evocative. The Sayings are arranged chronologically
under subject headings; where no precise date is given, the
quotation comes from Sayings of the Year. People's titles are
given as at the date of the Saying.

Some famous Sayings were missed at the time—Sir
Harold Wilson's 'A week is a long time in politics' is an
example. Sometimes shortage of space has resulted in a
significant omission, but to retrieve it a week later is against
the rules. Sadly, in wartime the Sayings disappeared for
months on end. There are gaps in 1918, 1919, 1940, 1941,
1942 and 1944 which disrupt the historical flow. Nevertheless
I hope the book highlights other aspects of our times, perhaps
not so well known.

I have often been asked how the Sayings are picked. The
answer is by reading—newspaper reports, magazine articles,
Hansard—and by listening to as much radio and television as
possible. It is a subjective process and no two compilers will
ever arrive at the same selection. *The Observer*'s editor, by
tradition, makes the final choice for publication.

Many early Sayings are not what today's compilers would
consider 'real' Sayings. They are often entertaining extracts
from articles written by G. K. Chesterton, Hilaire Belloc,

H. G. Wells or George Bernard Shaw. Sermons were a legitimate source. Throughout the 1920s and early 1930s Bishops, Deans and Reverends appear as often as politicians.

The Sayings are a good outlet for obsessions. W. R. Inge, Dean of St Paul's, had one on railway carriages: 'I wish that instead of reserving compartments for smokers the railway companies might label some carriages for "Talkers".' The question of having a car rather than a family exercised many Sayers in the 1930s when the first twinges of the consumer society were felt. Contemporary music is often criticised. 'Modern dance music is like a party of gorillas tearing up a wire mattress' said a Councillor Markwick from Hove in 1932.

Before World War II people were not inhibited about mentioning class. 'The poorest of the poor have not such bad bad teeth as the lower middle classes, because the poor have not the money to spend on sweets' observed Sir Frank Colyer in 1934. 'I have been told by many people that they were in favour of birth control, but did not want it for the working classes because where were the soldiers to come from?' reported a Mrs Lasky in 1925. Wherever the soldiers did come from, their wellbeing in wartime was hardly of paramount importance: 'Will the Rt Hon gentleman consider the waste of soldiers' time in cleaning their teeth?' asked Mr F. Montague in the House of Commons in 1942.

Good Sayings do not always—or even very often—come from famous people. More often the famous feel obliged to speak in weighty, stereotyped phrases, minding their ps and qs and conscious of being on the record. It is the unwatched words that usually make the most entertaining Sayings. Most of the Sayings in this book are by people who, when quoted by name, are recognised or easily remembered.

If there were awards for consistency in providing Sayings of quality for many years, they would go to Harold Macmillan and J. B. Priestley. Captain H. Macmillan was quoted in 1927, a year later than J. B. Priestley's first appearance on 7 November 1926. Both have had Sayings published in the 1970s. Though there are weeks when a compiler can shout 'Eureka', on the whole one has to agree with Lord Annan that 'The day of the jewelled epigram is past.'

I could not have compiled this book without the work of my predecessors, known and unknown, on *The Observer*. I should like to thank those of my colleagues who have produced Sayings for me over the years; and *The Observer*'s present editor, Donald Trelford, who encouraged me to tackle the book.

Valerie Ferguson, May 1978

The Arts

All the English history that I know was learned from the cinema.

Lord Baden-Powell, 7.10.1917

Vers libre seems to me to be merely *la prose enchaînée*.

Lord Darling, 27.11.1921

A deep tragedy lies behind a book. Do not believe novelists are pleased with their efforts. They only brazen their faces before the world.

Sir Hugh Walpole, 11.12.1921

Of what use is culture to a labourer?

Emanuel Shinwell, 25.2.1923

I am not interested in being regarded as a benefactor of mankind. I am an artist.

Jacob Epstein, 20.12.1931

Too often poets are not regarded until they have been fifty years in their graves. They bring their gifts of joy and ask bread from the world and the world, too late, gives them a memorial stone.

John Masefield, 25.9.1938

Judging from American plays and films, the virile American, whether taxi driver, political agent, or photographer, feels that to remove his hat indoors would be to doff his manhood.

Desmond MacCarthy, 18.12.1938

All the arts in America are a gigantic racket run by unscrupulous men for unhealthy women.

Sir Thomas Beecham, 5.5.1946

To write one's memoirs is to speak ill of everybody except oneself.

Marshal Pétain, 26.5.1946

Authors are easy enough to get on with—if you are fond of children.

Michael Joseph, 29.5.1949

It isn't enough to have the eyes of a gazelle; you also need the claws of a cat in order to capture your bird alive and play with it before you eat it and join its life to yours. This is the mystery of painting.

Augustus John, 5.11.1950

I know that poetry is indispensable, but to what I could not say.

Jean Cocteau, 23.10.1955

Why should people go out to see bad films when they can stay at home and see bad television?

Sam Goldwyn, 9.8.1956

Drama is life with the dull bits cut out.

Alfred Hitchcock, 10.7.1960

From Hollywood as well as Peking we have learned that power comes down the barrel of a gun.

Rev Don Cupitt, 20.9.1970

Bad Guesses

In my opinion the attempt to build up a Communist Republic on the lines of strongly centralised State Communism, under the iron rule of the dictatorship of a party, is ending in a failure.

Prince Kropotkin, 11.7.1920

I know of no method by which an aristocratic nation like England can become a democracy.

Hilaire Belloc, 20.2.1921

I do not think we shall hear much more of the general strike in our life.

Ramsay Macdonald, 28.5.1926

We are all satisfied in South Africa now.

General Jan Smuts, 12.12.1926

We have reached a point where we can look back and see that the Socialist movement in Western Europe has failed.

John Middleton Murry, 5.3.1933

Anyone who looks for a source of power in the transformation of the atom is talking moonshine.

Sir Ernest Rutherford, 17.9.1933

We are winning international respect.

Adolf Hitler, 21.1.1934

It is as certain as the day that a Labour town council, a Socialist or Communist government would not for a day tolerate strikes in social and other services necessary for the life of the nation.

George Lansbury, 6.5.1934

By this revolution the German form of life is definitely settled for the next thousand years.

Adolf Hitler, 9.9.1934

In ten years there will be no Belisha beacons. For if cars continue to be made at the same rate as now and with increasing cheapness there will be no pedestrians left.

Leslie Hore-Belisha, 17.3.1935

Colour and stereoscopy will make the cinema into the greatest art in the world. Bad films will be impossible.

John Betjeman, 7.4.1935

I do not believe in the probability of anything very much worse than mustard gas being produced.

Professor J B S Haldane, 17.10.1937

We shall reach the helm within five years.

Sir Oswald Mosley, 16.1.1938

The strike weapon is out of date.

Joseph Jones, Yorkshire Miners' Leader, 24.7.1938

The cession of any Colony or Protectorate—save as the result of a crushing defeat in war—is simply unthinkable and would never be accepted by the nation.

Lord Lugard, 27.11.1938

The Government has no reason to suppose that if grave events should supervene that they should supervene in a fortnight or three weeks or any particular time.

Neville Chamberlain, 30.7.1939

I ain't going to let no darkies and white folks segregate together in this town.

> *Eugene Connor, Police Commissioner of Birmingham, Alabama, USA,* 12.3.1950

In all likelihood world inflation is over.

> *Dr Per Jacobsson, Managing Director of the IMF,* 4.10.1959

We have stopped losing the war in Vietnam.

> *Robert McNamara, US Defense Secretary,* 5.12.1965

You won't have Nixon to kick around any more, gentlemen. This is my last Press conference.

> *Richard Nixon,* 2.11.1962

Writing about the Nixon Administration is about as exciting as covering the Prudential Life Assurance Company.

> *Art Buchwald,* 19.7.1970

We are determined to bring the rate of domestic inflation down by 10 per cent by the end of the next pay round and to single figures by the end of 1976.

> *Denis Healey,* 6.7.1975

Britain, the British Empire, the British . . .

Even if the three great democracies constituting the British Empire had only existed for one thing—for fighting in the Great War—the Empire would not have existed in vain.

> *Arthur Balfour,* 21.12.1919

The British Empire must behave like a gentleman.

> *David Lloyd George,* 21.8.1921

If you talk to the Englishman about class war, revolution, or things of that kind, he will tell you in forcible language that he has no use for foreign theories or foreign crimes.

> *Viscount Cave,* 26.4.1925

It pays in England to be a revolutionary and bible-smacker most of one's life—and then come round.

Lord Alfred Douglas, 17.7.1938

Mr Churchill need not worry about the future of Britain. I am looking after it.

Aneurin Bevan, 24.10.1948

The British public has always had an unerring taste for ungifted amateurs.

John Osborne, 10.3.1957

The British have a wonderful aptitude for inventing societies for the prevention of virtually anything. There is one consolation: they mostly fail to prevent anything.

Sir Arthur Norman, 15.2.1970

Churchill was fundamentally what the English call un-stable—by which they mean anybody who has that touch of genius which is inconvenient in normal times.

Harold Macmillan, 21.12.1975

Half the country is middle-class: the other half is trying to be.

Alan Ayckbourn, 20.3.1977

. . . and as others see us

It is equality of monotony which makes the strength of the British Isles.

Eleanor Roosevelt, 17.10.1948

England is, in some ways, the Yugoslavia of the West.

Jean-Jacques Servan-Schreiber, 6.2.1949

The most dangerous thing in the world is to make a friend of an Englishman, because he'll come sleep in your closet rather than spend ten shillings on a hotel.

Truman Capote, 25.3.1966

Broadcasting

I can see the nerve doctor of the future saying to the man with a nagging wife, 'Give her a radio set.'

Sir Eric Geddes, 29.8.1926

A timid BBC is an appalling prospect because, though timid, it will always be influential, and it will confirm thousands of us in our congenial habit of avoiding unwelcome truth.

E M Forster, 20.12.1931

Apparently the will of the people is that for three-quarters of the day the BBC shall relay the biggest nonsense to be heard in music.

Sir Thomas Beecham, 18.4.1937

The gift of broadcasting is, without question, the lowest human capacity to which any man could attain.

Harold Nicolson, 5.1.1947

The ideal voice for radio should have no substance, no sex, no owner, and a message of importance for every housewife.

Ed Murrow, 1.5.1949

Television has brought back murder into the home—where it belongs.

Alfred Hitchcock, 19.12.1965

Broadcasting is no longer a profession for gentlemen: the players have taken over.

Sir Hugh Greene, 25.8.1969

All my shows are great. Some of them are bad. But they are all great.

Sir Lew Grade, 14.9.1975

The Civil Service

The besetting sin of civil servants is to mix too much with each other.

Sir William Beveridge, 7.9.1924

You can cut any public expenditure except the Civil Service; those lads spent a hundred years learning to look after themselves.

Sir Richard Marsh, 19.9.1976

The Civil Service is a self–perpetuating oligarchy, and what better system is there?

Lord Armstrong, 8.5.1977

Communism

Communism might be likened to a race in which all competitors come in first, with no prizes.

Lord Inchcape, 12.7.1924

If Communism achieves a certain success, it will achieve it not as an improved economic technique but as a religion.

J M Keynes, 25.10.1925

Marx only became so influential because Lenin studied him.

Aldous Huxley, 30.6.1935

Communism I like, but Communist intellectuals are savages.

Jean-Paul Sartre, 25.3.1956

Definitions

Economy consists not in transferring the burden from one set of citizens to another, but in not spending the money.

Lord Robert Cecil, 23.7.1922

Statesmanship is housekeeping on a great scale.

Sir John Simon, 3.11.1922

The cinema may be described as a cross between a thought-saving machine and a cocktail.

John Galsworthy, 5.11.1922

A platitude is simply a truth repeated till people get tired of hearing it.

Stanley Baldwin, 1.6.1924

If a man is a pessimist he wears a belt as well as braces; if he is an optimist he wears neither.

Lord Dewar, 16.9.1924

A fanatic means a man whose faith in something he thinks true makes him forget his general love of truth.

G K Chesterton, 8.3.1925

A dictatorship is a confession of political incapacity and sloth in the governed.

Signor Francesco Nitti, 22.8.1926

Politics is the art of looking for trouble, finding it whether it exists or not, diagnosing it incorrectly, and applying the wrong remedy.

Sir Ernest Benn, 29.3.1930

A politician is a person with whose politics you don't agree. If you agree with him, he is a statesman.

David Lloyd George, 7.7.1935

Pornography is only a form of sentimentality.

Graham Greene, 5.12.1937

A major part of my life is spent in that state of resentful coma which at universities is called research.

Harold Laski, 23.1.1938

Nagging is constructive criticism too frequently repeated.

Percy Cudlipp, 13.11.1949

A diplomat is a man who can make his guests feel at home when he wishes they were at home.

Walter Gifford, US Ambassador to London, 15.7.1951

A prisoner of war is a man who tries to kill you and fails, and then asks you not to kill him.

Winston Churchill, 6.7.1952

Copying from one book is clearly cribbing; copying from two is research; and if one can get somebody else to do the copying this becomes a project.

F G G Carr, Director National Maritime Museum, Greenwich, 7.12.1952

A compromise is the art of dividing a cake in such a way that everyone believes that he has got the biggest piece.

Dr Ludwig Erhard, 28.12.1958

Nagging is the repetition of unpalatable truths.

Dr Edith Summerskill, 17.7.1960

A psychiatrist is a man who goes to the *Folies Bergère* and looks at the audience.

Dr Mervyn Stockwood, 15.10.1961

Moral indignation is in most cases 2 per cent moral, 48 per cent indignation and 50 per cent envy.

Vittorio de Sica, 17.12.1961

The difference between perseverance and obstinacy is that perseverance means a strong will and obstinacy means a strong won't.

Lord Dundee, 10.2.1963

Riots are the language of the unheard.

Dr Martin Luther King, 9.7.1969

The function of the expert is not to be more right than other people, but to be wrong for more sophisticated reasons.

Dr David Butler, 2.11.1969

A statesman is a politician who places himself at the service of the nation. A politician is a statesman who places the nation at his service.

Georges Pompidou, 1973

If you buy land on which is a slagheap 120 feet high and it costs £100,000 to remove it, that is not speculation, but land reclamation.

Harold Wilson, 7.4.1974

Politics is the art of acquiring, holding and wielding power.

Indira Gandhi, 4.5.1975

Middle age is when wherever you go on holiday you pack a sweater.

Denis Norden, 18.1.1976

As far as Socialism means anything, it must be about the wider distribution of smoked salmon and caviar.

Sir Richard Marsh, 10.10.1976

Unhappiness is best defined as the difference between our talents and our expectations.

Dr Edward de Bono, 12.6.1977

Economics and Economists

It is the business of the Treasury to turn down good proposals, accepting only the very best, because there can never be enough money to put all the good schemes into effect.

J M Keynes, 12.12.1920

The economists are generally right in their predictions, but generally a good deal out in their dates.

Sidney Webb, 25.2.1924

Before Keynes there were only three great economists—Adam Smith, who believed that God was behind economics, Ricardo, who believed that the devil was behind them; and Karl Marx, who believed they took it in turns but that the devil was on top at the moment.

Lord Pakenham, 7.4.1946

I have no doubt we will get out of the recession some time. When we do, no doubt the Prime Minister and others will tell us it is the greatest miracle since the loaves and the fishes.

Michael Foot, 8.10.1967

Unfortunately, good economics is not always perceived to be good politics.

William Simon, US Treasury Secretary, 10.10.1976

Education

Public education to be good must be education of the whole man and not entirely the raising of a bookworm.

H A L Fisher, 7.10.1917

If any institution is controlled and led by Etonians all will be well.

General Lord Plumer 25.5.1919

A great many people now reading and writing would be better employed in keeping rabbits.

Edith Sitwell, 13.5.1923

The Western World has rediscovered in the twentieth century the ancient truth that the business of popular education is neither formal teaching nor political enlightenment but direct social reconstruction.

Lord Eustace Percy, 4.6.1933

I often think how much easier the world would have been to manage if Herr Hitler and Signor Mussolini had been at Oxford.

Lord Halifax, 7.11.1937

There is no more sense in students participating in the management of universities than there would be in a union of housewives participating in the management of Marks and Spencer's stores.

Enoch Powell, 15.3.1970

Equality

Men are not born equal, and they are not born fraternal: and I will ask any mother in the audience if she does not agree with me.

Stanley Baldwin, 15.3.1925

Equality is a futile pursuit: equality of opportunity is a noble one.

Iain Macleod, 28.5.1969

We have been slow in accepting that a more equal society also means levelling down.

J K Galbraith, 11.5.1975

If your only opportunity is to be equal, then it is not equality.

Margaret Thatcher, 28.11.1976

Fashion

The smart new cliché of the moment usually masks something that was discussed threadbare in the streets of Ur.

Marjorie Bowen, 12.1.1930

It was said that in the Victorian days it took two sheep to clothe one woman: today all her clothing is provided from one silkworm.

Dowager Lady Swaythling, 23.5.1937

British women are rosy-cheeked and healthy, but somehow they can't seem to keep their stockings right.

Fiorello La Guardia, Mayor of New York, 19.7.1942

The trick of wearing mink is to look as though you were wearing a cloth coat. The trick of wearing a cloth coat is to look as though you are wearing mink.

Pierre Balmain, 25.12.1955

Food

Sound meals are not infrequently the foundation of sound morals.

Lord Henry Cavendish-Bentinck, 18.3.1919

I am inclined to think that only a hungry world can be a peaceful world. If the 450 million people of India were all well fed and prosperous they might not be pacific as they are now.

G V Jacks, Director of the Commonwealth Bureau of Soil Science, 14.2.1954

In one hundred years from now, I can imagine scampi being looked upon as an old English dish.

Sir Charles Forte, 29.5.1960

If I had the choice between smoked salmon and tinned salmon, I'd have it tinned. With vinegar.

Harold Wilson, 11.11.1962

The best number for a dinner party is two—myself and a damn good head waiter.

Nubar Gulbenkian, 19.12.1965

Freedom and Liberty

Freedom is a bourgeois notion devised as a cloak for the spectre of economic slavery.

V I Lenin, 11.7.1920

The truth is that men are tired of liberty.

Benito Mussolini, 8.4.1923

Freedom is when one hears the bell at 7 o'clock in the morning and knows it is the milkman and not the Gestapo.

Georges Bidault, 23.4.1950

If people have to choose between freedom and sandwiches, they will take sandwiches.

Lord Boyd-Orr, 7.8.1955

It is one of the ironies of our time that the techniques of a harsh and repressive system should be able to instill discipline and ardour in its servants—while the blessings of liberty have too often stood for privilege, materialism and a life of ease.

John F Kennedy, 5.2.1961

Liberty is conforming to the majority.

Hugh Scanlon, 14.8.1977

Futurology

General elections in future will tend to become wage auctions.

Sir Henry Fairfax-Lucy, 3.8.1919

Instead of burning 1,000 tons of coal, our descendants will take the energy out of an ounce or two of matter.

Sir Oliver Lodge, 14.12.1919

In one or two generations the nobility in England will be forced to go to work.

Gordon Selfridge, 3.4.1921

Communists who believed we could completely alter the economic form of society in three years were visionaries. I say it will take at least a century.

V I Lenin, 7.4.1921

The conquest of the air, so jubilantly hailed by general opinion, may turn out the most sinister event that ever befell us.

John Galsworthy, 4.11.1923

A world no better educated than this will never be very much better than this; it will be a world of race mobs and lynchings, of pogroms and race brigandage, of furious struggles for disputed territories, and wars and wars and wars.

H G Wells, 20.7.1924

Depend upon it, the Universe is ultimately intelligible, however complicated and hopeless it may appear.

Sir Oliver Lodge, 25.1.1925

Three modern inventions will lighten the task of the educator and the educational administrator—broadcasting, the motor car and the cinema.

H A L Fisher, 8.3.1925

What oil is doing today, coal will do again tomorrow.

Sir John Cadman, 21.6.1925

Photography is going to marry Miss Wireless, and heaven help everybody when they get married. Life will be very complicated.

Marcus Adams (Society Photographer), 6.9.1925

The inference to which I am led by my study is that England is heading rapidly toward an era of great revolutionary upheavals.

Leon Trotsky, 20.9.1925

I can imagine that the day may yet come when the last supporters of a discredited, antiquated and almost forgotten creed called Socialism will be a small group of noble lords deriving their titles from various sports in the Clyde Valley.

John Buchan, 10.7.1927

We may expect an era of internecine wars, comparable only to the invasions of Huns and Mongols in the Middle Ages.

Bertrand Russell, 21.8.1927

The removal of the perpetual fear of losing one's job is the greatest human problem that will have to be solved in the course of this century.

Lord Trent, 21.7.1935

It will take some time for the lesson of Spain to be learned, but increasingly it will be recognised that the Communist Party has ceased to be revolutionary.

Fenner Brockway, 30.5.1937

Each of us, to defend his own petroleum, is in the process of arranging to set fire to the entire Middle East.

Guy Mollet, 8.4.1956

We thought we could put the economy right in five years. We were wrong. It will probably take ten.

Anthony Wedgwood Benn, 22.4.1968

I see the time coming when people will regard it as a duty to use contraception rather than a duty not to.

Rt Rev Hugh Montefiore, 25.2.1970

By the end of 1991, it is not unreasonable to suppose, motoring will become an occupation indulged in by the super-rich, just as it was in the early 1920s.

Lord Tanlaw, 29.5.1977

Homespun Philosophy

Always decry the time in which you live; it is a proof of vitality.

Hilaire Belloc, 18.1.1920

A man does not care for applause or recognition except when he is not sure he is working on the right lines.

W R Inge, Dean of St Paul's, 11.7.1920

Love your neighbour is not merely sound Christianity; it is good business.

David Lloyd George, 20.2.1921

The pace that kills is the crawl.

Lord Leverhulme, 15.5.1921

A half-truth, like half a brick is always more forcible as an argument than a whole one.

Stephen Leacock, 16.10.1921

The extremist diminishes in his influence, in number and power, and in the degree that he reaches a stage of responsibility.

J R Clynes, 29.1.1922

I have never known anybody who worked too hard, though I have known many who think they do.

Lord Hewart, 1.7.1923

It is fatal to be appreciated in one's own time.

Osbert Sitwell, 10.2.1924

The gift of rhetoric has been responsible for more blood-shed on this earth than all the guns and explosives that were ever invented.

Stanley Baldwin, 16.3.1924

People who jump to conclusions rarely alight on them.

Philip Guedalla, 30.3.1924

Too often the strong silent man is silent only because he does not know what to say and is reputed strong only because he has remained silent.

Winston Churchill, 29.6.1924

You cannot ask one Utopian to live in another's Utopia.

G K Chesterton, 17.8.1924

It is easy to settle the world on a soap box.

David Lloyd George, 26.10.1924

It is quite an arguable proposition that mankind has owed as much to its bugbears as to its heroes.

Winston Churchill, 25.1.1925

Most people would die sooner than think: in fact they do so.

Bertrand Russell, 12.7.1925

Every time thought is driven underground, even if it is bad thought, it is a danger to society.

Ramsay Macdonald, 6.12.1925

Luck and destiny are the excuses of the world's failures.

Henry Ford, 6.3.1927

Everybody is somebody's bore.

Edith Sitwell, 3.7.1927

Destroy him as you will, the bourgeois always bounces up —execute him, expropriate him, starve him out en masse, and he reappears in your children.

Cyril Connolly, 7.3.1937

23

People with an over-abundance of dignity and an over-supply of power have always in the end been targets for laughter.

Charlie Chaplin, 12.2.1939

The 'isms' of our time are really substitute religions, margarine beliefs.

J B Priestley, 20.8.1939

If two men on the same job agree all the time, then one is useless. If they disagree all the time, then both are useless.

Darryl Zanuck, 23.10.1949

There are occasions when dirty linen does need washing in public because it is the only way of convincing the unthinking that it exists.

Earl Winterton, 18.12.1949

If A is success in life, then A equals X plus Y plus Z. Work is X; Y is play; and Z is keeping your mouth shut.

Professor Albert Einstein, 15.1.1950

Gratitude, like love, is never a dependable international emotion.

Joseph Alsop, 30.11.1952

It is important when you haven't got any ammunition to have a butt on your rifle.

Sir Winston Churchill, 31.1.1954

Laughter would be bereaved if snobbery died.

Peter Ustinov, 13.3.1955

I think that bad philosophers may have a certain influence, good philosophers—never.

Bertrand Russell, 24.4.1955

I take the view, and always have done, that if you cannot say what you have to say in twenty minutes you should go away and write a book about it.

Lord Brabazon, 26.6.1955

If a man has good manners and is not afraid of other people, he will get by even if he is stupid.

Sir David Eccles, 25.12.1955

It is no good shutting your eyes and saying British is Best three times a day after meals, and expecting it to be so.

The Duke of Edinburgh, 29.4.1956

Ashes to ashes and clay to clay; if the enemy don't get you, your own folk may.

James Thurber, 1.7.1956

A saint may embrace poverty, but national poverty won't breed a race of saints.

Sir Miles Thomas, 17.2.1957

When you are skinning your customers, you should leave some skin on to grow so that you can skin them again.

Nikita Khruschev, 28.5.1961

Manners are especially the need of the plain. The pretty can get away with anything.

Evelyn Waugh, 15.4.1962

The moment you have protected an individual you have protected society.

Dr Kenneth Kaunda, 6.5.1962

The weak have one weapon: the errors of those who think they are strong.

Georges Bidault, 15.7.1962

I have often found that a man who trusts nobody is apt to be the kind of man that nobody trusts.

Harold Macmillan, 22.12.1963

If you live among wolves you have to act like a wolf.

Nikita Khruschev, 20.9.1964

If you feed people just with revolutionary slogans they will listen today, they will listen tomorrow, they will listen the day after tomorrow but on the fourth day they will say 'To hell with you'.

Nikita Khruschev, 27.9.1964

If we should promise people nothing better than only revolution, they would scratch their heads and say: 'Is it not better to have good goulash?'

Nikita Khruschev, 27.12.1964

The man who first abused his fellows with swear-words instead of bashing his brains out with a club should be counted among those who laid the foundations of civilisation.

Professor John Cohen, 21.11.1965

No one is born prejudiced against others, but everyone is born prejudiced in favour of himself.

Dr David Stafford Clark, 1.5.1966

The whole point about getting things done is knowing what to leave undone.

Stella, Lady Reading, 14.8.1966

'Mind you, I've said nothing'—I wouldn't like that to be my epitaph.

Conor Cruise O'Brien, 1.6.1969

It is never too late to admit that the job is harder when you've got to do it than what it seemed like when you were telling the other chap how to do it.

Vic Feather, 13.9.1970

You don't lead people by following them, but by saying what they want to follow.

Enoch Powell, 6.12.1970

History teaches us that men and nations behave wisely once they have exhausted all other alternatives.

Abba Eban, 20.12.1970

Nothing is surely a waste of time when one enjoys the day.

Arthur Koestler, 8.10.1972

We must learn to distinguish morality from moralising.

Dr Henry Kissinger, 24.10.1976

The saddest illusion of revolutionary socialists is that revolution will itself transform the nature of human beings.

Shirley Williams, 23.1.1977

Political morality is a long way from church morality.

Andrew Young, US Ambassador to the UN, 27.3.1977

Industry and Work

Punctuality, regularity, discipline, industry, thoroughness, are a set of 'slave' virtues.

G D H Cole, 1.1.1922

The general strike has taught the working classes more in four days than years of talking could have done.

Arthur Balfour, 14.11.1926

It is impossible in the present order of society to secure the optimum level of output and employment by any other means except by paying the capitalist his full rate and, if anything, a little over.

J M Keynes, 10.11.1929

Whenever you save five shillings you put a man out of work for a day.

J M Keynes, 18.1.1931

To help the unemployed is not the same thing as dealing with unemployment.

Sir Herbert Samuel, 19.2.1933

The men always want more wages. I should be very sorry to see them stop doing it.

Ernest Bevin, 26.11.1933

Enterprise doesn't have to be private in order to be enterprise.

Herbert Morrison, 27.12.1942

Right now the basic insecurity the workers feel is this: they are haunted by the spectre of the van driving up to the door to take away the TV set.

Bessie Braddock, 19.6.1955

I look forward to the day when there is a strike not because a firm has introduced automation, but because it has not.

Jo Grimond, 30.9.1956

It's a recession when your neighbour loses his job: it's a depression when you lose yours.

Harry S Truman, 13.4.1958

One man's wage rise is another man's price increase.

Harold Wilson, 11.1.1970

In developing our industrial strategy for the period ahead we have the benefit of much experience. Almost everything has been tried at least once.

Anthony Wedgwood Benn, 17.3.1974

The biggest differential of all is between the man in a job and the man who is out of one.

James Callaghan, 6.3.1977

Ireland

There has always been in Ireland a good deal of what I may call rhetorical and contingent belligerency.

H H Asquith, 28.10.1917

Apart from political trouble, Ireland is the most peaceful country in the world.

J R Devlin, 4.5.1919

Such words as 'The Republic' 'Independence' and 'The Memory of the Dead' can bring a lump into the throat of most Irishmen but really modern political problems cannot be solved by lumps in the throat.

George Bernard Shaw, 1.1.1922

The Irish people do not gladly suffer common sense.

Oliver St John Gogarty, 9.5.1935

We have flower battles just as they do in Nice. Only here we throw the pots as well.

Brendan Behan (on the Dublin Festival), 10.7.1960

It is a short step from the throwing of paving stones to the laying of tombstones.

Terence O'Neill, 12.11.1969

Israel

We in Israel are not only an international problem. We are also a reality in our own right—a social and a cultural and a historic dream.

Abba Eban, 1.3.1970

I consider peace more important than territory.

David Ben-Gurion, 31.5.1970

I've never had to kill anyone. I'm not saying it with relief. There's no difference between one's killing and making decisions that will send others to kill.

Golda Meir, 1.4.1973

Law and Lawyers

I cannot help thinking that the English Bar is probably the oldest and tightest trade union in the world.

Sir Patrick Hastings, 21.5.1921

For the game of advocacy you want a good digestion, a good temper, and a good clerk. And of these three the greatest is a good clerk.

Sir John Simon, 5.12.1926

No one has ever yet been able to find a way of depriving a British jury of its privilege of returning a perverse verdict.

Lord Chief Justice Goddard, 20.2.1955

Two hundred years ago we made a practice of treating lunatics as criminals. Nowadays we are more inclined to treat criminals as lunatics.

Lady Wootton, 8.7.1962

Mercy is not what every criminal is entitled to. What he is entitled to is justice.

Lord Hailsham, 14.2.1975

I think that a judge should be looked on rather as a sphinx than as a person—you shouldn't be able to imagine a judge having a bath.

Judge H C Leon, 21.12.1975

Life and Living

There is only one form of the simple life—living at the Ritz Hotel and touching the bell.

Cecil Roberts, 18.10.1936

The luxuries of one generation become the necessities of the next.

Lord De La Warr, 15.5.1938

One of the minor pleasures in life is to be slightly ill.

Harold Nicolson, 22.1.1950

It's not worth giving dinner parties at Blenheim. The State dining-room is on show, and our dining-room only holds thirty.

The Duchess of Marlborough, 26.7.1953

Love and Marriage

I would warn the wives of eminent men to treat their husbands as if they were not eminent.

A Clutton Brock, MP, 25.3.1919

Marriage to many people appears to be nothing but a necessary preliminary step towards being divorced.

Mr Justice Darling, 9.5.1920

A girl who thinks that a man will treat her better after marriage than before is a fool.

William Clarke Hall, 19.9.1920

Bigamy is not a vice of wealth, the rich can find other less illegal outlets for their emotions.

Lord Buckmaster, 15.10.1922

A loving wife is better than making 50 at cricket or even 99; beyond that I will not go.

Sir James Barrie, 7.6.1925

A man does not buy his wife a fur coat to keep her warm, but to keep her pleasant.

Sir Seymour Hicks, 24.11.1946

There are only about 20 murders a year in London and not all are serious—some are just husbands killing their wives.

Commander G H Hatherill of Scotland Yard, 21.2.1954

An archaeologist is the best husband any women can have: the older she gets the more he is interested in her.

Agatha Christie, 2.1.1955

Happy is the man with a wife to tell him what to do and a secretary to do it.

Lord Mancroft, 18.12.1966

It's better to be unfaithful than faithful without wanting to be.

Brigitte Bardot, 29.12.1968

How else do you get on in this world except by marrying well?

Nigel Dempster, 3.4.1977

Medicine

I like dining with the medical profession, for it is agreeable to find out that mine is not the only profession that does not always practise what it preaches.

Dean Inge, 1.11.1925

Men

I always think that one of the great charms of my sex is that the best of us remain boys to the end.

Stanley Baldwin, 20.1.1929

Men can allow themselves to run to seed in the most appalling fashion. Women tolerate it because they think they are not entitled to ask for anything more.

Germaine Greer, 25.10.1970

Never despise what it says in the women's magazines: it may not be subtle but neither are men.

Zsa-Zsa Gabor, 11.4.1976

Miauw!

Just imagine Sophocles, Euripides, Shakespeare, Johnson, Molière, Webster, Ford, Congreve, Sheridan, Ibsen, Strindberg and a few others gathered together having a chinwag about the drama: and then imagine Patrick Braybrooke* hurrying up to them, holding Noel Coward by the hand, and saying, 'Scuse me boys, but I want to introduce a master dramatist to you all!'

Sean O'Casey, 19.1.1936

As usual the Liberals offer a mixture of sound and original ideas. Unfortunately none of the sound ideas is original and none of the original ideas is sound.

Harold Macmillan, 24.12.1961

I am sure Mr Heath thinks he is honest. But I wish he didn't have to have his friends to say it so often.

Roy Jenkins, 31.5.1970

I do not often attack the Labour Party. They do it so well themselves.

Edward Heath, 10.6.1973

Milestones

We have recognised that it is for the good of the country that we should abdicate the Crown of the Russian state, and lay down the supreme power.

Tsar Alexander II of Russia, 18.3.1917

I, Woodrow Wilson, President of the United States of America, do hereby proclaim to all whom it may concern that a state of war exists between the United States and the Imperial German Government.

Woodrow Wilson, 18.4.1917

Men will return from the front feeling that after their great sacrifice they cannot be satisfied with a country that is not substantially better than before they went.

Christopher Addison, 16.12.1917

* Patrick Braybrooke was the first biographer of Noel Coward

I am scarcely less free than I was before, for have I not been a prisoner all my life?

ex-Tsar Alexander II of Russia, 24.6.1917

The German flag is to be hauled at 3.57 today (Thursday), and is not to be hoisted again without permission.

Sir David Beatty, 24.11.1918

We are at the beginning of a long period of serious political and social disorder and our age is essentially one of transition, alike from the political, economic and social points of view.

Dr Eduard Benes (of Czechoslovakia), 20.8.1933

Let the Nazis come on. We are not afraid.

Dr Engelbert Dollfuss, Austrian Chancellor, 18.2.1934

Let us never forget this—since the day of the air the old frontiers are gone. When you think of the defence of England you no longer think of the chalk cliffs of Dover, you think of the Rhine.

Stanley Baldwin, 5.8.1934

There used to be a limitation on the number of false teeth a recruit could have. I have removed that limitation.

Leslie Hore-Belisha, 14.11.1937

Because of the achievements in the National-Socialist cause, Upper Austria is to have the special distinction of having a concentration camp.

Gauleiter Eingruber, 2.4.1938

It is said abroad that we are so disagreeable. We always spring our surprises at weekends when Cabinet Ministers are out of town.

Dr Josef Goebbels, 10.4.1938

We in Poland do not understand the conception of 'peace at any price'.

Colonel Josef Beck, 7.5.1939

The German march into Prague opened the eyes of the blind, made the deaf to hear, and even, in some places, made the dumb speak.

Winston Churchill, 21.5.1939

Those who remember the relative prosperity of the last war had better forget it.

Sir William Beveridge, 14.1.1940

The 1918 mind lost us Singapore.

Major General Gordon Bennett, 8.3.1942

Anyone who draws rations for a person who is not living with them, and uses the rations personally, will go to prison. So far as I am concerned it is a form of unpatriotic gluttony.

Claud Mullins, 8.3.1942

It has been stated that a large number of international crooks are coming to London for the Coronation, and that some of them are actually installed in hotels, disguised as hotel proprietors.

Emrys Hughes, 29.2.1953

We know how to repel pirates.

President Nasser, 5.8.1956

We are not at war with Egypt. We are in armed conflict.

Sir Anthony Eden, 4.11.1956

I do not know how many we shot . . . It all started when hordes of natives surrounded the police station. If they do these things they must learn their lesson the hard way.

Colonel Pienaar, Area Police Commander (after the Sharpeville shooting), 27.3.1960

The US must be willing to continue bombing until every work of man in North Vietnam is gone.

General Curtis Le May, 6.10.1968

That's one small step for man, one giant leap for all mankind.

Neil Armstrong, 21.7.1969

In the bad old days communities were said to be divided by inequalities of class. This has now virtually disappeared but in its place there has appeared segregation by age group.

The Duke of Edinburgh, 18.1.1970

Our Vietnam is neither in Moscow, nor in Peking, Havana or Belgrade. It is in Chile.

Dr Salvador Allende, 1.11.1970

I wanted to be an up-to-date King. But I didn't have much time.

The Duke of Windsor (Edward VIII), 1972

The era of low-cost energy is almost dead. Popeye is running out of spinach.

Peter Peterson US Secretary of Commerce, 19.11.1972

The industrial nations will have to realise that this era of terrific progress and even more terrific wealth based on cheap oil is finished.

The Shah of Iran, 30.12.1973

This company is not bust. We are merely in a cyclical decline.

Lord Stokes (when Chairman of British Leyland), 1974

Modesty

I occasionally swank a little because people like it; a modest man is such a nuisance.

George Bernard Shaw, 7.3.1937

It is not often that Ministers are modest.

Herbert Morrison, 24.10.1943

However tired people may be of me, I think most people in the country will regard me as the lesser of two evils. I always put these things in a modest way.

Harold Wilson, 26.4.1970

I think it is fair to say that my own estimate of myself may be at variance with some of my critics.

Dr Henry Kissinger, 1974

Money

My gold came from God.

John D Rockefeller, 12.3.1933

There's not enough money in the world.

William Randolph Hearst, 24.6.1934

Nobody who has wealth to distribute ever omits himself.

Leon Trotsky, 23.3.1937

If you can actually count your money, then you are not really a rich man.

John Paul Getty, 3.11.1957

Music and Musicians

I go back to Bach as a sick dog instinctively grubs at the roots and herbs that are its right medicine.

Pablo Casals, 27.11.1921

My advice to all who want to attend a lecture on music is 'Don't; go to a concert instead'.

Ralph Vaughan Williams, 7.1.1923

Nationalisation

Under national ownership, if the employer were a competent man he might get a job on the managerial staff, but if he were not he might have to go and work as a collier.

G D H Cole, 4.5.1919

Nationalisation will be the Magna Carta of the twentieth century.

H G Wells, 7.3.1920

Some of our people have the idea that when nationalisation comes a man can do what he likes. That is not our idea.

Arthur Horner, (*when National Production Officer of the NUM*), 9.9.1945

We'll find it very difficult to explain to the voters that simply by taking over Marks and Spencer we can make it as efficient as the Co-op.

Harold Wilson, 27.5.1973

On the Record

It is brought home to me with every day that I pass at my work that Europe is moving uneasily, slowly it may be, but certainly to a new catastrophe.

Austen Chamberlain,
(when Secretary of State for Foreign Affairs), 12.4.1925

One must do the greatest good one can for one's friends and the utmost harm to one's enemies.

Benito Mussolini, 24.5.1925

I do not believe that right alone is enough; one must also have might.

Adolf Hitler, 3.1.1932

I believe that Providence has chosen me for a great work.

Adolf Hitler, 11.9.1932

I ask you to judge me by the enemies I have made.

Franklin D Roosevelt, 16.10.1932

We want war with no nation.

Yosuke Matsuoka (Japanese Foreign Minister,
1940–1), 27.11.1932

We have been tolerant with the Jews, but just let them look out. I warn them for the last time.

Dr Josef Goebbels, 13.5.1934

If Wales is to be governed by a nation outside our land, I would prefer to be governed from Dublin.

Gwynfor Evans, 31.10.1948

I was an expert on migration problems.

Adolf Eichmann, 25.1.1961

I believe that this nation should commit itself to achieving the goal, before this decade is out, of landing a man on the moon and returning him safely to earth.

John F Kennedy, 28.5.1961

I am afraid that a lot of the things that many of us have said in the past three years are going to have to be unsaid.

Denis Healey, 1968

I think that probably the attacks on me in the Press and in politics have been worse than any other Prime Minister has had to face—even Lloyd George.

Harold Wilson, 16.3.1969

If South Africa wants to oppress the black people within its boundaries by force of arms and also to attack neighbouring black States, I wish to make it very clear that we do not even require threepence worth of gunpower for that.

John Vorster, 20.9.1970

I am proud of everything the Irgun fighters did.

Menachem Begin, 16.1.1972

I have never been an idealist—that implies you aren't going to achieve something.

Arthur Scargill, 1974

Parliament—House of Commons

There is a vast amount of humbug in the House of Commons but it really does very little harm because we know that it is humbug.

Arthur Hopkinson, 23.3.1919

There are three golden rules for Parliamentary speakers: 'Stand up. Speak up. Shut up'.

The Speaker, J W Lowther, 25.5.1919

I believe we would turn out much better work in the House of Commons if we did two hours digging every day.

David Lloyd George, 8.6.1924

A Parliament elected by the universal suffrage of voters grouped according to geographical areas is about as truly representative as a bottle of Bovril is a true representative of an ox.

Eleanor Rathbone, 29.3.1931

If from any speech in the House one begins to see any results within five to ten years after it has been delivered, one will have done very well indeed.

Robert Boothby, 8.3.1936

Some MPs talk a lot. Few listen.

Sir Ian Fraser, 2.8.1942

A great many persons are able to become members of this House without losing their insignificance.

Beverley Baxter, 3.11.1946

Parliament—House of Lords

The one great advantage in the House of Lords is that it is as unlike the House of Commons as it can possibly be.

Lord Willoughby de Broke, 27.4.1919

The British House of Lords is the British Outer Mongolia for retired politicians.

Anthony Wedgwood Benn, 4.2.1962

Think of it, a second chamber selected by the whips—a seraglio of eunuchs!

Michael Foot, 9.2.1969

The House of Lords is a perfect eventide home.

Lady Stocks, 4.10.1970

Patriotism

If people are going to drink champagne, the larger the share of taxation on that wine the greater will be their patriotism.

Austen Chamberlain, 2.5.1920

'My country, right or wrong' is an insult hurled at God.

Jerome K Jerome, 19.12.1920

The single most important impediment to global institutions is the concept of 'My country right or wrong'.

U Thant, 2.1.1972

We may not be the greatest at winning Winter Olympics but at least we can carry our bloody flag properly.

Squadron Leader Mike Freeman, bobsleigher and flag bearer at the Winter Olympic Games, 6.2.1972

Pious Hopes

Our aim is that the kind of justice which Germany has meted out to Belgium shall in future be impossible upon this planet. Nothing else matters in comparison.

Lord Milner, 30.9.1917

The lessons of the past six years should be enough to convince everybody of the danger of nations striding up and down the earth armed to the teeth.

General John J Pershing, 2.1.1921

The bonds, social, economic, industrial and commercial, which are always drawing North and South Ireland together, will prove too powerful for the bigots and revolutionaries.

J R Devlin, 17.8.1924

England is at last ripe for revolution.

Leon Trotsky, 21.6.1925

We hope and expect to see an Indian Union, strong and united.

Sir Stafford Cripps, 5.4.1942

We see ourselves as a true white State in Southern Africa, with a possibility of granting a full future to the black man in our midst.

Dr Hendrik Verwoerd, 7.2.1960

There are going to be no dramatic changes in Rhodesia.

Ian Smith, 5.1.1975

I believe that once people realise they will be better off with a low pay limit than a higher one, they will see the sense of it.

Denis Healey, 11.4.1976

Plus ça Change . . .

Twenty years ago the British Press was without a rival in the world for its good tone and truthfulness. That is no longer so.

Sir Gilbert Murray, 7.1.1917

There is a dreadful fallacy fermenting in men's minds that all they want is higher wages.

Sir Auckland Geddes, 12.10.1919

I do not believe you could point to any case where men work better for the State than they work for syndicates.

David Lloyd George, 12.10.1919

This Government will soon be in the position of Rabelais, whose will consisted of this sentence: 'I have nothing, I owe much, and the rest I leave to the poor.'

Herbert Samuel, 19.10.1919

When the State endeavours to function as a charitable institution it does more harm than good.

Arthur Hopkinson, 20.2.1921

The Government will go on with patience and courage until the last revolver is picked out of the hands of the last assassin in Ireland.

Sir Hamar Greenwood (when Secretary for Ireland), 29.5.1921

Ancient civilisations were destroyed by the imported barbarians; we breed our own.

Dean Inge, 15.10.1922

It is not enough to cater for people who have a thirst for education; we must coerce the teetotaller.

Father Ronald Knox, 20.7.1924

I sometimes wonder whether the British traveller does really need a seat.

E C Cox (of the Southern Railway Co), 31.10.1926

There is too often today a tendency for trade unions to abuse their powers.

J H Thomas, 31.10.1926

It is probably true that far more people in this country
can tell you the name of the Tottenham Hotspur centre-
forward than can tell you the name of the Archbishop of
York.

Mr Justice MacKinnon, 2.2.1930

As a rule, the motor-cycle is driven by a hot-headed
youth, without a hat, his hair flowing down behind; and
everybody, except the young lady on the pillion behind
him, hates him.

Mr Justice Swift, 8.2.1931

The young man today is compelled by circumstances
beyond his control to become a robot in a fatalistic scheme
of things which must cause him to believe that he counts
for very little.

Ernest Bevin, 7.1.1934

It is difficult for the foreigner to understand why Britain
pays young able-bodied men the dole to do nothing when
the country needs soldiers.

Alfred Duff Cooper, 21.6.1936

We should have been able to reduce the price of gas by
now but for the effect of the inflationary spiral, but for the
increase in the cost of coal and other commodities, and
but for the increase in wages.

G Le B Diamond, Chairman,
West Midlands Gas Board, 28.2.1954

There is really no future in importing extra materials
that we cannot afford in order to turn them into extra
goods that we do not export.

Harold Macmillan, 22.4.1956

When the ruins of Pompeii were uncovered, dice were
found. It is a sad commentary on the unvarying conditions
of human nature that some of those dice were loaded.

Lord Kilmuir, 29.5.1960

Politics and Politicians

All Governments are pretty much alike, with a tendency on the part of the last to be worst.

Austen Chamberlain, 1.6.1919

To terrorise a country is not to govern it.

J R Clynes, 13.7.1919

English experience indicates that when the two great political parties agree about something it is generally wrong.

G K Chesterton, 16.11.1919

The art of government wants more character than brains.

T E Lawrence, 25.7.1920

Frighten the people of this country until they frighten the Government; that is the only way to get anything done.

Admiral Mark Kerr, 11.2.1923

'Sunshine for your grandchildren' is a bad electoral programme.

David Lloyd George, 4.3.1923

You cannot govern nations without a mailed fist and an iron will.

Benito Mussolini, 11.5.1924

There are three classes which need sanctuary more than others—birds, wild flowers, and Prime Ministers.

Stanley Baldwin, 24.5.1925

It is no use having a thermometer which is near the radiator, and that is the trouble with all those political and industrial thermometers in London.

David Lloyd George, 5.9.1926

A continued progression to the Left, a sort of inevitable landslide into the abyss, is the characteristic of all revolutions.

Winston Churchill, 23.1.1927

There is just as much security in a political agreement as in a regiment of soldiers or a fleet of battleships.

Ramsay Macdonald, 8.9.1929

I am afraid Mr Baldwin will never make a great leader as he seems to have a congenital incapacity for playing a dirty game.

Captain Wedgwood Benn, 10.11.1929

I hate elections, but you have got to have them; they are medicine.

Stanley Baldwin, 11.10.1931

The politicians and financiers seem to me to be the plumbers of the modern world—always going back to the country for something they haven't got and always pretending it is only the absence of that particular imple-ment which prevents them from doing their job.

A P Herbert, 3.1.1932

It is amazing how wise great statesmen can be when it is ten years too late.

David Lloyd George, 8.5.1932

Dictators have only become possible through the invention of the microphone.

Sir Thomas Inskip, 18.10.1936

If the Prime Minister does not trust the people, the people will not trust the Prime Minister.

The Duke of Montrose, 29.11.1936

The Labour Party should be something more than an alms-house for retired agitators.

J M Keynes, 29.1.1939

Government by postponement is bad enough, but it is far better than government by desperation.

Adlai Stevenson, 27.12.1953

Exhortation to other people to do something is the last resort of politicians who are at a loss to know what to do themselves.

Paul Chambers, 12.11.1961

We shall not totter either to the Right or to the Left: let them totter to us.

Lord Rea, 26.9.1965

A little nonsense now and then is not a bad thing. Where would we politicians be if we were not allowed to talk it sometimes?

Enoch Powell, 19.12.1965

The professional politician can sympathise with the professional advertiser. Both must resign themselves to a low public estimation of their veracity and sincerity.

Enoch Powell, 19.12.1965

Politics should be fun—politicians have no right to be pompous or po-faced. The moment politics become dull, democracy is in danger.

Lord Hailsham, 3.4.1966

There are times in politics when you must be on the right side and lose.

Professor J K Galbraith, 1968

The first requirement of a statesman is that he be dull. This is not always easy to achieve.

Dean Acheson, 21.6.1970

Throughout history rulers have invoked secrecy regarding their actions in order to enslave citizens.

Senator Sam Irvin, 15.5.1973

If politicians lived on praise and thanks, they'd be forced into some other line of business.

Edward Heath, 30.9.1973

A government big enough to give you everything you want is a government big enough to take from you everything you have.

Gerald Ford, 18.1.1974

As I learnt very early on in my life in Whitehall, the acid test of any political decision is the question: 'What is the alternative?'

Lord Trend, 21.12.1975

Politics is like boxing—you try to knock out your opponent.

President Idi Amin, 18.1.1976

Poverty

The real poor mostly wear black clothes.

Dean Inge, 3.8.1919

Poor people always lean forward when they speak because they want people to listen to them. Rich people can sit back.

Michael Caine, 4.9.1966

It needs to be said that the poor are poor because they don't have enough money.

Sir Keith Joseph, 1.3.1970

The Press

I only read articles attacking me: never those that praise— they are too dangerous.

Georges Clemenceau, 27.3.1921

The history of journalism suggests that the ambition to start a newspaper is widespread, perennial, and generally foolish.

Lord Sands, 2.3.1924

Nearly every man thinks he can do three things, namely, run a newspaper, build a fire and guide the Government wisely.

Gordon Selfridge, 15.6.1924

The life of a newspaper editor resembles the discouraging eternity of those who, in hell, try to fill sieves with water.

Aldous Huxley, 7.6.1925

Manners change so rapidly, indeed, that it would not be at all surprising to see a newspaper nowadays referring to Mr Baldwin and Mr Chamberlain as Stanley and Neville —or even as Stan and Nev.

Robert Lynd, 9.5.1937

It is part of the social mission of every great newspaper to provide a refuge and a home for the largest possible number of salaried eccentrics.

Lord Thomson, 22.11.1959

Tribune itself occasionally reminds me of an old-style drab Co-op shop nervously displaying a few cocktail sausages.

Dennis Potter, writing in Tribune, 13.6.1960

A good newspaper, I suppose, is a nation talking to itself.

Arthur Miller, 26.11.1961

On the whole I would not say that our Press was obscene. I would say it trembles on the brink of obscenity.

Lord Longford, 2.6.1963

'and the Press said . . . '

History is not fit to be read unless by those who realise it is a branch of indecent literature.

New Statesman, 30.12.1917

No one is entirely useless. Even the worst of us can serve as horrible examples.

Editor, State Prison Newspaper, Salt Lake City, 23.1.1949

The best defence against the atom bomb is not to be there when it goes off.

The British Army Journal, 20.2.1949

Psychologists and Psychology

The psychologist is a great advance on the mid-Victorian phrenologist, but not perhaps such a great advance as he would like us to think.

Lord Leverhulme, 29.4.1923

Race

The chief danger to the white man arises from his arrogant contempt for other races.

Dean Inge, 27.2.1921

The white man must no longer dominate the coloured man, even for his own good.

Lord Willingdon, 11.10.1925

For every voice in Britain calling for a policy to Keep Britain White, there is a corresponding call to Keep Africa Black.

Dr Kenneth Kaunda, 21.7.1968

One shop steward is worth a thousand social workers in the field of race relations.

Dr David Pitt, 4.10.1970

Religion

The Church should be no longer satisfied to represent only the Conservative Party at prayer.

Maud Royden, 22.7.1917

Religion for me is merely opium for the intellect.

Leon Trotsky, 2.7.1920

The proper function of the clergy is not to make a better world to live in, but better people to live in the world.

Rt Rev Arthur Perowne, Bishop of Bradford, 14.1.1923

There is something wrong with a man if he does not want to break the Ten Commandments.

G K Chesterton, 12.4.1925

The Church of England has never been famous for its friendliness to other people. The Church has always been a sort of refrigerator van on the back of the train.

Rt Rev Edward Lowry Henderson, Dean of Salisbury, 29.5.1938

Confirmation—one of the sacraments of the Church of England—tends to be a sort of spiritual sheep dip.

Lord Altrincham, 22.6.1938

Science and Technology

Every advance in science leaves morality in its ancient balance; and it depends still on the inscrutable soul of man whether any discovery is mainly a benefit or mainly a calamity.

G K Chesterton, 2.4.1922

I also am a revolutionary, though only a scientific one.

Professor Albert Einstein, 4.3.1923

There is by no means the same certainty today as a decade ago that the atoms of an element contain hidden sources of energy.

Sir Ernest Rutherford, 16.9.1923

The destiny of mankind has slipped (we are all aware of it) from the hands of politicians into the hands of scientists.

Desmond MacCarthy, 8.5.1931

The only thing that science has done for man in the last hundred years is to create for him fresh moral problems.

Most Rev Geoffrey Fisher,
Archbishop of Canterbury, 22.1.1950

The discovery of nuclear chain reaction need not bring about the destruction of mankind any more than did the discovery of matches.

Albert Einstein, 9.3.1952

It is a distinction between science and technology that technology must always be useful whereas science need not be.

Sir Patrick Linstead, 3.1.1965

If sunbeams were weapons of war we would have had solar energy long ago.

Sir George Porter, 21.8.1973

Scientists never advertise their failures.

Dr Sydney Brenner, Medical Research Council,
Cambridge University, 19.9.1976

Sex

The sexual impulse, in its widest form, was a very great impulse towards the building of the Panama Canal.

D H Lawrence, 16.9.1923

Sex is a playground for lonely scientists.

Dr Carl Jung, 6.10.1935

Shadows Before

An armed nation has in the end to fight, and 'the end' comes within a period of half a century.

Ramsay Macdonald, 25.2.1923

At the present moment, which may prove to be the eve of another Armageddon, we are not ready.

Lord Rothermere, 17.6.1934

Concentration camps cannot be sanatoriums.

Hermann Goering, 16.12.1934

We can do without butter, but not without guns.

Dr Josef Goebbels, 19.1.1936

Germany represents the danger, and the only danger, of a European war in the future.

Lord Eustace Percy, 5.4.1936

Germany cannot renounce her claim for a solution of her colonial demands.

Adolf Hitler, 13.9.1936

Germany's new air force is not a peace parade instrument.

Hermann Goering, 6.3.1938

Liberals must give up being so excessively respectable. We have got to have some bloody noses in the party.

Jo Grimond, 16.11.1958

The question is no longer to know if Africa will be liberated, but rather with whose aid and against whose will that liberation will be carried out.

Sekou Touré, President of Guinea, 13.12.1959

The plea for security could well become a cloak for errors, misjudgments and other failings of government.

Richard Nixon, 14.5.1961

I will not resign. I declare my will to resist by every means, even at the cost of my life.

Salvador Allende, 16.9.1973

Signs of the Times

It is now possible to hear the purest cockney spoken in first–class railway carriages.

William Pett Ridge, 28.3.1920

If I were on a jury I would never find a person guilty of murdering a cook-general.

Edgar Wallace, 13.12.1925

An Englishman today would need a good deal of moral independence to be seen reading a Bible in a crowded railway carriage.

John Drinkwater, 30.6.1929

Any contemporary of ours who wants peace and comfort before anything has chosen a bad time to be born.

Leon Trotsky, 26.3.1933

Go to the docks and you will see there quiet little girls doing work which a Negro would probably describe as a hard day's work.

Brendan Bracken, 30.8.1942

It is now bad form to appear in clothes that look too new.

Hugh Dalton, 8.11.1942

Is it not a fact that in many districts people are being left without their only retainer?

Lord Lyle of Westbourne, 29.11.1942

I think cigar bands are hardly necessary in total war.

Judge Finnemore, 7.3.1943

The modern stocking will go into a spontaneous ladder if you merely wink at it.

Sir Ian Fraser, 25.4.1943

NAAFI canteens have boiled sweets as well as brilliantine—all the luxuries.

Mr Justice Humphreys, 18.7.1943

It is perfectly plain that a bath is very largely a luxury.

Lord Maugham, 30.4.1944

Extra food is allowed for weddings, golden weddings, funerals, and other festivities.

Dr Edith Summerskill, 30.1.1949

Now we are in a period which I can characterise as a period of cold peace.

Trygve Lie, 21.8.1949

Most of us have stopped using silver for every day.

Margaret Thatcher, 2.8.1970

I have only large brown eggs. There are no large white ones because of the three-day week.

Express Dairy employee, 20.1.1974

Concorde is the finest plane in the world. Concorde is not dead.

Anthony Wedgwood Benn, 24.3.1974

A fair price for oil is whatever you can get plus ten per cent.

Dr Ali Ahmed Attiga of OPEC, 12.5.1974

Better a three-day week than a no-day week.

Edward Heath, 28.7.1974

My wife answered the telephone and on being asked who she was she rightly said she was the Duchess of Norfolk. 'What's that?' she was asked, 'a pub?' That's what being a Duke means today.

The Duke of Norfolk, 15.5.1977

South Africa

I have often said to myself that the history of South Africa is the one true and great romance of modern history.

General Smuts, 27.5.1917

Don't forget that unlike the French, unlike the British and unlike the Portuguese, we Afrikaners have no other place to go.

Roelof Botha, 29.5.1977

Soviet Union

Mr Balfour may perhaps be permitted to observe that he never for a moment questioned the complete efficacy of Soviet methods for making rich men poor; it is in the more difficult and, in Mr Balfour's view, more important task of making poor men rich that failure is to be found.

Arthur Balfour, 5.9.192c

Communism will pass away from Russia, but it will have lighted a torch for the world of workers not readily to be extinguished.

Maxim Gorki, 9.10.1921

The foreign newspapers ought to be ashamed of themselves for expressing disapproval of the recent shooting of a few score of anti–Soviet terrorists.

Vyatcheslav Mikhailovich Molotov, 3.2.1925

There are no unemployed either in Russia or in Dartmoor jail, and for the same reason.

Philip Snowden, 3.7.1932

It would be a mistake to think that everything is quite all right in our country.

Josef Stalin, 15.1.1933

Gaiety is the most outstanding feature of the Soviet Union.

Josef Stalin, 24.11.1935

To attempt to export revolution is nonsense.

Josef Stalin, 8.3.1936

Russia is a riddle wrapped in a mystery inside an enigma.

Winston Churchill, 1.10.1939

Russian Communism is the illegitimate child of Karl Marx and Catherine the Great.

Clement Attlee, 15.4.1956

Soviet aid is given not with strings but with a rope.

Richard Nixon, 15.7.1956

Perhaps the greatest tragedy of the Communist Revolution is that it began in Russia: the Russians merely adapted all the evil forces of the Tsars and use them till this day.

Arnosht Kolman, on resigning from the Soviet Communist Party after 58 years, 10.10.1976

Speeches

If half the people who make speeches would make concrete floors they would be doing more good.

Lord Darling, 15.7.1917

Speeches on social occasions ought to be like ladies' skirts —long enough to cover the subject and short enough to be interesting.

Lord Weir, 19.12.1919

Spontaneous speeches are seldom worth the paper they are written on.

Leslie Henson, 17.1.1943

The human brain starts working the moment you are born and never stops until you stand up to speak in public.

Sir George Jessel, 7.8.1949

After-dinner speaking should be like oil prospecting. If you don't make a strike, stop boring.

Sir Miles Thomas, 25.11.1956

I do not object to people looking at their watches when I am speaking. But I strongly object when they start shaking them to make certain they are still going.

Lord Birkett, 30.10.1960

I think people really will concede that on this of all days
I should begin my speech with the words 'My husband
and I'.

> *Queen Elizabeth II (on her 25th wedding anniversary),*
> 20.11.1972

Sport

As soon as money comes into sport, honour begins to go
out of it.

> *Rt Rev James Edward Cowell Welldon, Dean of Durham,*
> 16.10.1921

Games are the last recourse to those who do not know how
to idle.

> *Robert Lynd,* 1.4.1923

You get to know more of the character of a man in a round
of golf than you can get to know in six months with only
political experience.

> *David Lloyd George,* 27.1.1924

I am getting to an age when I can only enjoy the last
sport left. It is called 'hunting for your spectacles'.

> *Lord Grey of Falloden,* 20.11.1927

Much of the trouble in Russia, politics apart, is due,
I believe, to the fact that Russia is not a games playing
nation.

> *W W Wakefield,* 18.3.1928

The Derby does much to foster the vein of optimism and
stoicism in disappointment which is so important a feature
of the national character.

> *Major J Astor,* 31.5.1936

When we were children we asked my Uncle Charles what
it was like to play cricket with W G Grace. 'The dirtiest
neck I ever kept wicket behind' was his crisp reply.

> *Lord Chandos,* 21.6.1959

There is one great similarity between music and cricket.
There are slow movements in both.

> *Sir Neville Cardus,* 31.12.1967

Soccer in England is a grey game, played on grey days, watched by grey people.

Rodney Marsh, 18.9.1977

Taxes

A miner would rather be ten shillings out of pocket by not doing a day's work than earn ten shillings and pay 2/4d of it as income tax.

Clem Edwards, 3.8.1919

There is no such thing as a good tax.

Winston Churchill, 6.6.1937

To tax and to please is no more given to man than to love and be wise.

Sir John Simon, 1.5.1938

Taxation should be an energiser, not a penaliser.

James Callaghan, 3.3.1963

It is no part of the State's duty to facilitate the spiritual redemption of rich men by impoverishing them in this life.

John Grigg, 27.6.1964

The Chancellor is not like Robin Hood, taking wealth from the rich and giving it to the poor. He is taking it from the rich and giving it to the sheriff.

John Pardoe, 21.12.1975

Chancellors have relied upon inflation to be their best tax collectors.

Sir William Pile, 27.2.1977

Theatres and Players

Theatrical managers have two deadly foes to fight in this country, which are not to be found in any other country in the world—Puritanism and Philistinism.

H B Irving, 6.5.1917

Actors and actresses are so busy trying to be ladies and gentlemen and golfers that they have no time left to pay attention to their jobs.

Osbert Sitwell, 5.9.1926

'Hamlet', if written today, would probably be called 'The Strange Affair at Elsinore'.

Sir James Barrie, 28.4.1929

A play that will not last forty years and be all the better for it is not worth writing.

George Bernard Shaw, 24.1.1937

I still prefer a good juggler to a bad Hamlet.

Charles B Cochran, 3.10.1943

The art of acting consists in keeping people from coughing.

Ralph Richardson, 19.1.1947

If a playwright is funny the English look for the serious message, and if he is serious they look for the joke.

Sacha Guitry, 19.5.1953

An actor's a guy who, if you ain't talking about him, ain't listening.

Marlon Brando, 1.1.1956

That's what show business is—sincere insincerity.

Benny Hill, 12.6.1977

Trade Unions

If trade unionism is in danger it is through the action of extreme men in its own ranks.

David Lloyd George, 10.8.1919

The most conservative man in the world is the British trade unionist when you want to change him.

Ernest Bevin, 11.9.1927

Had the employers of past generations dealt fairly with men, there would have been no trade unions.

Stanley Baldwin, 18.1.1931

While we may believe all men are brethren, we strongly object to any big brother trying to push us around.

Jack Tanner, President of the TUC, 12.9.1954

The shop steward is a little like an egg. If you keep him in hot water long enough he gets hard-boiled.

Jack Tanner, 12.9.1954

If we wear the winter woollies of traditional trade unionism against the hot sun of automation, we may sweat it out instead of thinking it out.

Sir Harry Douglass, 13.9.1964

I always expect someone to tell us that the original martyrs of the trade union cause were all members of the Tolpuddle Conservative and Unionist Association.

Michael Foot, 6.4.1969

The motto of 'every man for himself' was taken down from the wall when the first trade union was formed.

Len Murray, 11.9.1977

If trade unions hold the whip hand, upon whose back does the lash fall?

Margaret Thatcher, 29.9.1977

Travel

An Englishman's real ambition is to get a railway compartment to himself.

Ian Hay, 29.4.1923

Railway travelling is the best possible school of human patience.

Father Ronald Knox, 1.11.1925

We can at least encourage our undesirables to join tourist parties to Spain, where they will doubtless be adequately dealt with by the local purgers.

Rose Macaulay, 28.7.1936

Travelling by air is demoralising. You are treated like a gentleman.

Kingsley Martin, 26.6.1949

The flights, landings and take-off of airships called 'flying saucers' and 'flying cigars' of any nationality are forbidden on the territory of the community of Châteauneuf-du-Pape.

Decree by the Mayor of Châteauneuf-du-Pape, 31.10.1954

United States of America

We never were and never will be able to maintain isolation.

President Warren Harding, 29.5.1921

The White House is the finest jail in the world.

President Harry S Truman, 7.11.1948

The President spends most of his time kissing people on the cheek to get them to do what they ought do without getting kissed.

President Harry S Truman, 6.2.1949

To make a United Europe, we need the help of the best Europeans of all—the Americans.

Dr Konrad Adenauer, 4.12.1949

When I was in the White House I used to keep on my desk a sign which said 'The buck stops here'.

President Harry S Truman, 4.9.1955

I reject the cynical view that politics is inevitably, or even usually, dirty business.

President Richard Nixon, 19.8.1973

There can be no whitewash at the White House.

President Richard Nixon, 30.12.1973

Vengeance

Vengeance as a policy has nowhere and at no time proved the path to wisdom.

The Chief Rabbi, Dr J A Hertz, 22.2.1920

The days when Jewish blood can be shed unavenged are past.

Menachem Begin, 13.11.1977

War and Peace

In war time no soldier is free to say what he thinks: after the war no one cares what a soldier thinks.

General Sir Ian Hamilton, 23.12.1917

Only by adequate preparation for war can peace in any way be guaranteed.

Sir Douglas Haig, 15.6.1919

As long as there is mankind there will be wars. Only dreamers believe otherwise.

Field Marshal Hindenburg, 3.8.1919

I do not know whether war is an interlude in peace or peace an interlude to war.

Georges Clemenceau, 19.10.1919

People who talk about peace are very often the most quarrelsome.

Lady Astor, 11.5.1924

Take the profits out of war and you will assist the movement to end war before war ends us.

Bernard Baruch, 12.7.1925

We hear war called murder. It is not: it is suicide.

Ramsay Macdonald, 4.5.1930

Air power may either end war or end civilisation.

Winston Churchill, 19.3.1933

The great commander must have a touch of the gambler.

Major-General A P Wavell, 8.12.1935

I cannot subscribe to the idea that it might be possible to dig ourselves in and make no preparation for anything other than passive defence. It is the theory of the turtle, which is disproved at every Lord Mayor's banquet.

Winston Churchill, 8.1.1939

War is always stimulating to affairs of the heart.

Charles Dana Gibson, 27.6.1943

The next war will be fought with atom bombs and the one after that with spears.

Professor Harold Urey, 29.12.1946

The way to win an atomic war is to make sure it never starts.

General Omar Bradley, 20.4.1952

If it is said that we cannot afford another war like Korea, the answer is that such a war is the only kind that we or anyone else can afford.

Dean Acheson, 4.4.1954

The only alternative to co–existence is co–destruction.

Pandit Nehru, 29.8.1954

The ability to get to the verge without getting into the war is the necessary art.

John Foster Dulles, 15.1.1956

War is a very rough game but I think politics is worse.

Field Marshal Lord Montgomery, 30.12.1956

Rule One of the book of war is: Don't march on Moscow.

Field Marshal Lord Montgomery, 2.6.1962

History is littered with wars which everybody knew would never happen.

Enoch Powell, 22.10.1967

War is the most exciting and dramatic thing in life. In fighting to death you feel terribly relaxed when you manage to come through.

General Moshe Dayan, 13.2.1972

Women

Women must come off the pedestal. Men put us up there to get us out of the way.

Lady Rhondda, 12.12.1920

There has been a softening in the use of the English language in connection with persons of the other sex. Female teachers are now alluded to in Acts of Parliament as women teachers.

Chuter Ede, 11.2.1945

Too many homes are built on foundations of crushed women.

Clough Williams-Ellis, 1.12.1946

For every woman trying to free women there are probably two trying to restrict someone else's freedom.

Brigid Brophy, 25.10.1970

Long-legged girls are fascinating—built for walking through grass.

Laurie Lee, 10.7.1977

Ah, Youth

A person under twenty-five years of age is almost always very critical. I believe that is at the root of the progress of the human race.

Lord Hugh Cecil, 29.4.1917

Youth would be an ideal state if it came a little later in life.

Lord Asquith, 15.4.1923

Index